D0803256

American Indian
Art and Culture

COMANCHE

Heather Kissock

WEIGL PUBLISHERS INC.

"Creating Inspired Learning"
www.weigl.com

Published by Weigl Publishers Inc.
350 5th Avenue, 59th Floor
New York, NY 10118

Website: www.weigl.com

Library of Congress Cataloging-in-Publication Data

Kissock, Heather.
 Comanche : American Indian art and culture / Heather Kissock.
    p. cm.
 Includes index.   55736200   8/14
 ISBN 978-1-60596-988-6 (hardcover : alk. paper) -- ISBN 978-1-60596-989-3 (softcover : alk. paper) -- ISBN 978-1-60596-990-9 (e-book)
 1. Comanche art--Juvenile literature. 2. Comanche Indians--Material culture--Juvenile literature. 3. Comanche Indians--Social life and customs--Juvenile literature. I. Title.
 E99.C85K5 2011
 978.004'974572--dc22
                              2010005336

Printed in the United States of America in North Mankato, Minnesota
1 2 3 4 5 6 7 8 9 0 14 13 12 11 10

042010
WEP264000

Photograph and Text Credits
Cover: Courtesy, National Museum of the American Indian, Smithsonian Institution (02/1617); Alamy: pages 5, 7, 13, 16, 20; Canadian Museum of Civilization: page 23 (VI-D-84 a, b); Corbis: pages 4, 6; Getty Images: 10, 11, 12, 14, 15; Courtesy, National Museum of the American Indian, Smithsonian Institution: pages 8 (2/1803), 9M (23/288), 9B (2/1501), 21 (022585Bd); Nativestock: pages 9T, 17.

Every reasonable effort has been made to trace ownership and to obtain permission to reprint copyright material. The publishers would be pleased to have any errors or omissions brought to their attention so that they may be corrected in subsequent printings.

All of the Internet URLs given in the book were valid at the time of publication. However, due to the dynamic nature of the Internet, some addresses may have changed, or sites may have ceased to exist since publication. While the author and publisher regret any inconvenience this may cause readers, no responsibility for any such changes can be accepted by either the author or the publisher.

PROJECT COORDINATOR Heather Kissock

DESIGN Terry Paulhus

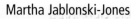

ILLUSTRATOR Martha Jablonski-Jones

Contents

The People

The Comanche Indians live on the southern plains of the United States. This is an area that stretches from Wyoming to northwest Texas. It includes the states of Kansas, Colorado, Oklahoma, and New Mexico.

The Comanche originally came from Wyoming. They began living in Texas in the 1700s. They first settled in the area around Palo Duro Canyon, in the state's panhandle. Later, they moved south to the central part of the state.

Today, there are about 14,500 Comanche living in the United States. Most reside in Oklahoma.

NET LINK
Find out what the Comanche call themselves at **www.comancheindian.com**.

Comanche Homes

TEEPEES

In the past, the Comanche lived in large teepees. A teepee was a cone-shaped house. It was made of wooden poles that were covered with bison hides.

Comanche Ideas

Comanche women were responsible for tanning the animal hides. Tanning is the process that turns hides into leather.

Inside the teepee, a fire pit was used for cooking and to create warmth. The smoke escaped through an opening at the top of the teepee.

Comanche Clothing

DRESSES

Women wore long deerskin dresses. The dresses often had fringes and were sometimes painted with Comanche designs. These designs often included stripes and **geometric** patterns.

BREECHCLOTHS, LEGGINGS, AND SHIRTS

Comanche men wore breechcloths made of bison hide or buckskin. They only wore shirts when the weather was cold or when they were going to battle. Then, their shirts were made from animal hide and often had important Comanche symbols painted on them. In colder weather, Comanche men also wore robes made from bison hides.

HEADWEAR

Some Comanche men wore headdresses that had eagle feathers trailing from the back. When men went to battle, they often wore a hat made from the fur on a bison's head. The horns were left attached.

JEWELRY

Most men had pierced ears and wore earrings made from shells. The Comanche also wore other jewelry, such as necklaces and belts.

MOCCASINS

Both men and women wore moccasins on their feet. Women also wore tall boots that stretched to the hip. These boots were made of either buckskin or bison hide.

Hunting and Gathering

BISON

Bison was the main part of the Comanche diet. Bison were usually hunted in the summer and fall months.

ROOTS

Root vegetables, such as parsnips, grew throughout Comanche lands. Women were responsible for digging them from the ground.

POTATOES

Like root vegetables, potatoes grew throughout Comanche lands. These were dug up and cooked.

Long ago, the Comanche were known as hunter-gatherers. This is because they hunted for meat and gathered plants found in nature. Later, when horses were brought to the area, the Comanche began relying on hunting more than gathering.

BERRIES

Comanche women gathered berries, such as mulberries, that grew in the area. They used the berries to flavor meat.

DEER

When bison were scarce, the Comanche would hunt deer. Deer was used for both food and clothing.

PECANS

The Comanche ate pecans for the energy they provided. Pecan tree leaves were used to treat **ringworm**.

Comanche Tools

BOWS AND ARROWS

The most important tool of the Comanche was the bow and arrow. Bows were made from wood and animal **sinew**. Arrows were made from wood and feathers. The Comanche used bows and arrows to hunt bison.

Comanche Ideas

Comanche men were excellent horsemen. While riding a horse at full gallop, they could lean over and shoot arrows at their prey from under the horse's neck.

BISON

The Comanche used bison to make many of their tools. Bison tails, for example, were used to make whips and fly swatters. Bison bones were used to make sewing needles and knives.

Moving from Place to Place

TRAVOIS When moving from place to place, the Comanche used a travois to carry their belongings. A travois was a type of sled. It was made of two poles that were joined by a platform.

Comanche Ideas

The Comanche used the poles from teepees to build their travois.

Long ago, a travois was pulled by a dog. When Europeans brought horses to the area, the Comanche began to use horses to pull their travois.

Comanche Music and Dance

The Comanche perform a variety of dances. In the past, people danced to prepare for war. Today, they dance to tell stories and to remember the past. These dances are often performed at events called **powwows**.

Drums are played to provide a beat for the dancers. Dancers sometimes carry rattles made from rawhide and shake them while they dance.
Songs are sung while the dancers perform.

THE DANCE

NET LINK

Watch Comanche dancers perform at
www.youtube.com/watch?v=9rC5Cqdypsg.

The Release of the Bison

Long ago, all of the world's bison were owned by an old woman and her young cousin. They kept the bison locked up on a farm and never shared them with anyone.

This made Coyote mad. He took a plan to the Comanche. He noticed that the cousin did not have a pet of his own. He told the Comanche that he would change himself into a dog and become the boy's pet.

The Comanche liked the idea and thought it would work. Coyote quickly turned himself into a dog and put himself in the path of the young boy. When the boy saw the dog, he picked it up and took it back to his mother. He asked if he could keep the dog. She said he could as long as he kept it in the pen with the bison. The dog was not to come in the house.

The boy agreed and placed the dog with the bison. When night fell, Coyote unlocked the door of the pen and began barking. The bison became scared and ran out of the pen. This is how bison came to wander the plains of North America.

Comanche Art

Bison was used in all parts of Comanche life, including their art. Bison hides often were painted with patterns that were important to the Comanche. These hides were then used as teepee covers, clothing, and other items.

The Comanche painted pictures and patterns on their faces and bodies. Clay and berry juice were used to make the paint.

Sometimes, the Comanche decorated their clothing with beadwork. Comanche beadwork was known for its bright colors and geometric designs.

Make a Drum and Mallet

Materials

2 balloons
an embroidery ring or other
   circular frame
2 elastic bands
a piece of cloth

stick or branch (0.5 inches in
   diameter and
   12 inches long)
paints for decorating
   (optional)

Steps
1. Cut off the bottom of one of the balloons.
2. Stretch the balloon over the top of the frame, and secure it with an elastic band.
3. Decorate the drum using the paints.
4. Cut off the bottom from the other balloon. Stuff the cloth into the end of the balloon to make a small ball.
5. Place the stick halfway inside the stuffed balloon. Gather the ends of the balloon around the stick, and fasten them with the other elastic band.
6. Now, your drum and mallet are ready to make music.

Glossary

geometric: featuring straight lines, circles, triangles, and other shapes

powwows: festivals that have singing, dancing, and drumming

ringworm: a disease that makes ring-shaped patches appear on the skin

sinew: tough fiber that joins muscle to bone

Index